# Discovering God's Plan

Understanding God's Will for Your Life

Copyright © 2021 by Gene Jennings

All rights reserved. No portion of this book may be reproduced in any form without the written permission from the author or publisher.

All Scripture cited is from the *Holy Bible, New International Version*® unless otherwise noted. Copyright © 1973, 1978, 1984 by International Bible Society. All rights reserved.

Scripture quotations marked NLT are taken from the *Holy Bible, New Living Translation*, copyright © 1996. Used by permission of Tyndale House Publishers, Inc. Wheaton, Illinois 60189. All rights reserved.

Scripture quotations marked NASB are taken from *The New American Standard Bible*, copyright © The Lockman Foundation, 1971, 1977, 1995. All rights reserved.

ISBN 9798735965503

First printing, April 2021

Cover design by ikukoyidesign

Late Night Press, North Augusta, SC
Printed in the U.S.A.

# Dedication

To my grandchildren, Elijah, Emersyn, Sanders, Kinsley, and one to be named soon. My prayer is that you will discover and live out God's dreams for your lives.

# Table of Contents

Chapter 1: Runnin' Down A Dream — 7

Chapter 2: What's On God's Mind? — 11

Chapter 3: Be A Follower — 17

Chapter 4: Be Filled — 23

Chapter 5: Be Fruitful — 31

Chapter 6: Be A Faithful Servant — 37

Chapter 7: Putting It All Together: Freedom — 47

Chapter 8: More Than You Could Ask Or Imagine — 55

Notes — 59

About the Author — 61

CHAPTER 1

# RUNNIN' DOWN A DREAM

I was on the verge of taking the 1990's by storm in the church world. A recent graduate of the largest seminary in the world and a newly appointed missionary to North America, the ministry ball had been placed on a tee for me, and I was ready to drive it down the middle of the theological fairway further than anyone else in my graduating class. I remember riding down the road late one night after making a few door-to-door evangelistic visits in a new subdivision in the metro Atlanta area. I was cruising in our 1982 Toyota Celica GT with the windows down and Tom Petty and the Heartbreakers cranked up in the cassette deck. I was singing and dreaming about the large church I was going to start. There would be hundreds - no, thousands of people coming to my church. Lives would be touched. Multitudes saved. A city transformed by the gospel.

I was singing it loud. Praying. Hoping. Knowing God would answer.

# DISCOVERING GOD'S PLAN

Runnin' down a dream.
Never would come to me.
Workin' on a mystery.
Going wherever it leads.

Baby boomers were changing the way we did church. Organs were giving in to guitars on Sunday mornings, and pianos were being replaced by electronic keyboards. The Boomers grew up on rock and roll, and they decided they'd rather have a band lead worship than a choir. And while they were at it, they changed the dress code. More suits were staying in the closet on Sundays, and jeans began to become acceptable worship attire.

I knew all of this, of course, and the new church that I had been assigned to start by our missions agency was going to rock the metro Atlanta region. I just knew it. I was runnin' down a dream.

Only, like Tom Petty sang, it never would come to me.

At least, not at that church and not in Atlanta.

I shared an office with David, another fellow pastor. We were called church planters because we were to plant new churches in the rapidly growing Atlanta area. He was on the south side of the city. I was on the north side. We used to dream about what our churches would become. I remember a day when David had a vision that he would like to start a service with someone singing "From A Distance (God is Watching Us)" a popular song by Bette Midler at the time.

"Wouldn't it be great?" David asked. "We could take a popular song that the churched and unchurched people would know and teach a spiritual lesson from it?"

I remember sitting in David's office thinking, "Man, that would be so cool." A Bette Midler song in a Sunday service.

I was truly running down a dream. I'd read about some new churches in Chicago and California that discarded organs, choir robes, and dress codes. Churches that strived to be more relevant in their music and teaching styles. Churches that had a heart for the unchurched and strived to make the gospel easier to digest and understand. I was ready to bring that style of church to Georgia.

But before my dreams came true, I had to discover God's dream for my life.

CHAPTER 2

# WHAT'S ON GOD'S MIND?

It's only natural. We focus on our dreams. We think our dreams are bigger and better than God's dreams - if we even think of God's dreams for us at all. However, the truth is God's dreams for our lives are much greater than our dreams. Our dreams are limited by time and space. Our dreams are carved out of our finite, selfish brains.

But God's dreams. Oh my friend! God has dreams for you that you cannot fathom. His dreams for us are beyond our imagination. God's dreams for our lives aren't even on our radars.

God's dreams are big. He's got great adventures in mind for you. If this is so, doesn't it make sense that we find out what's on God's mind? Shouldn't we delve into his Word and discover his will for our lives?

> God's dreams for our lives are much
> greater than our dreams!

But first, let's get one thing out of the way. I'm not talking about the American Dream. The American Dream is not necessarily God's dream for your life. The American Dream is a happy way of living achieved by a good education, hard work, and a little luck. It's a stable job, a spacious house, two late-model cars, plenty of money, a few kids, and a retirement plan to provide a nest egg for your later years.

But God's dream for your life has nothing to do with material things. God's dream for you doesn't involve mortgages, landscaping, Roth IRA's, or diapers. God's dream for your life is not about what you have. It's about who you are.

Many people ask, "How can I know God's will for my life?" First of all, we must understand that there is another question that needs to be answered before that question. The first question should be, "What is God's will?" Once you understand God's will, then you can get specific and ask, "What is God's will for my life?"

Sometimes we talk about finding God's will like it's lost. It's not lost. It's not like we're searching for buried treasure. It's right in front of us. God is not playing games with us. He is not playing hide and seek with you. God wants you to know and do his will more than you do! He's more committed to you than you are!

---

> Once you understand God's will, then you can get specific and ask, "What is God's will for my life?"

---

The truth is some people don't want to know God's will because they don't want to do it. And that is sad because living the life that God designed for you is so much more fulfilling than living life by your design.

Some people are afraid to know God's will because they think God is going to make them do something they don't want to do - something radical. A football player is afraid that God might make him become a ballerina. An introvert might be afraid that God will make her speak in front of large crowds. Someone who hates math might be afraid that God will want them to be an accountant. It rarely works that way. God can take your personality, your likes, your dislikes, your gifts, your abilities, and your talents and put you right in your sweet spot if you will let him.

I am convinced that knowing God's will for your life is much simpler than we have made it out to be.

Can you really find out what career God would have you seek? Can you really know what college to attend? Can you really know if a business decision is right? Can you really discover what God would have you do in retirement? Can you really know if a person is the right person to marry? Can God help us answer specific questions like these?

YES - but it may not work like you think.

When I was a new believer, I heard people say, "The answers to all of your questions are in the Bible." I always thought, "I'd like to know who's going to win the Super Bowl next year." All of my money problems would be solved!

I used to think I could find the answers to every question hidden in the Old Testament prophets. When I was a senior in high school, I was thinking about playing baseball at Newberry College in South Carolina. One night in my search for God's will, I decided to look to the Bible for an answer. I randomly opened my Bible and placed my index finger on a verse of Scripture. (Note: I do not recommend this method.) My finger landed on Isaiah 55:1 - "Come, buy wine and milk without money and without cost." I began to meditate on this verse. The Scripture said to "buy wine." What is wine made of? Berries. If you buy wine, that implies that it is new wine. New berry. Isaiah then mentions milk. There are lots of dairy farms in the area where Newberry College is located. Isaiah completes the verse writing "without money and without cost." Free!

It seemed obvious. God was telling me through Isaiah 55:1 that I would go to Newberry College on a baseball scholarship!

Sadly. That did not happen and that was not God speaking to me. It was something I had conjured up in my mind using terrible Biblical interpretation skills.

God wants you to find his will. Where do you suppose we will find it? In his Word, the Bible. But not like I tried to do. He makes it much more obvious and easier to understand.

We need to know what the Bible says about God's will and how it applies to our lives. There are four principles to follow. The first four are easy to understand but not always easy to do. The fifth point may be one of the most liberating things you've ever heard!

CHAPTER 3

# BE A FOLLOWER

Each spring there are hundreds of commencement speeches on high school and college campuses. Most of the speakers are leaders in their fields. They've achieved success in business, industry, the military, or athletics. The speakers often encourage graduates to become leaders for their generation. Don't just be a follower, they might say, set a new standard for those around you. Have high aspirations. Attain incredible goals. Focus on leading those around you to the greatest pinnacles of achievement possible.

Be a leader not a follower.

Truthfully, that's not bad advice. It makes for a wonderful commencement speech. When a hometown boy from Anytown, USA who became a celebrated astronaut speaks at his alma mater, people listen. "If he can do it, I can too," some graduates will say to themselves. When a former gymnast who won an Olympic gold medal stands behind the podium to share her story of success to a group of high school graduates, they are certain that it is possible, even plausible, that if they worked hard enough and studied long enough that maybe, just maybe, they could become a leader in their chosen field of study too.

There's nothing wrong with being a leader. But first, God wants you to be a follower.

Specifically, God wants you to follow Christ.

> *This is good, and pleases God our Savior, who wants all people to be saved and to come to a knowledge of the truth.*
>
> *- 1 Timothy 2:3-4*

> *Then he said to them all: "Whoever wants to be my disciple must deny themselves and take up their cross daily and follow me. For whoever wants to save their life will lose it, but whoever loses their life for me will save it. What good is it for someone to gain the whole world, and yet lose or forfeit their very self?"*
>
> *- Luke 9:23-25*

Throughout the New Testament gospels, Jesus said, "Come, follow me." I believe choosing to follow Christ is the most important decision a human being can make. In fact, C.S. Lewis wrote that Christianity, "if false, is of no importance, and, if true, of infinite importance. The one thing it cannot be is moderately important."

What does it mean to follow Jesus and how does one make that decision?

The word "saved" is what I call a "church word." It's a word typically used in a Sunday morning message or Bible study lesson. What does it mean to be saved? Simply put, we place our faith in the Savior, Jesus Christ, who died in our place for our sins, and we follow him.

---

> C.S. Lewis wrote that Christianity, "if false, is of no importance, and, if true, of infinite importance. The one thing it cannot be is moderately important."

---

We are sinners. Everyone has sinned. We are born with a selfish, sinful nature. If you don't believe that, have children. Before I became a father, I knew the Bible said we are all sinners (Romans 3:23). I knew it for a fact when my first child was born. As my son became a toddler, he would grab things and take things and say things like, "Mine!" or "I want that" or "Me!"

I remember at one point being dumbfounded by that. We didn't teach my son to be selfish. Where did this self-centeredness come from?

The Bible calls it our sinful nature. We are born with a bent toward self. If you take a few minutes to write down every sin you can think of, you would see that the root of all sin is selfishness. Why do we lie? To make ourselves look better than what we really are. Why do we steal? Because we want something for ourselves. Why do we gossip? Because we love to feel like we know something others don't know. It makes us feel important.

Because we are sinners and God is holy, God cannot have a relationship with us. It's like trying to mix oil and water. Sin creates a chasm between us and God. We need to be rescued, i.e., saved from our sins.

Jesus Christ died on the cross for our sins to bridge the gap between our sin and God's holiness. When we admit that we are sinners, believe that Jesus Christ died in our place, and commit our lives to follow him, we are saved.

This is God's ultimate demonstration of grace. This is why the hymn *Amazing Grace* is such a timeless song. God's grace is truly amazing!

And God wants us to truly follow him - not just apply for fire and life insurance. Following Jesus requires us to follow him as Savior and Lord. He saves us from our sinful, selfish ways and as Lord he guides us through our daily challenges. Too many believers treat Jesus like they're going through a cafeteria line. When you walk through a cafeteria line there are dozens and dozens of choices, i.e., salads, fruit, meat, vegetables, and desserts. You can't possibly eat everything so you kindly ask the server at each station for the food items you desire.

Many Christians have looked at their spiritual choices and said, "I'd like Jesus as Savior. I want to go to heaven. But I think I'll pass on his Lordship. I'll be the boss of my own life, thank you."

That is not God's best for you. Jesus is Savior AND Lord. They go together. He saves us from our sin, and he leads us like a shepherd in our everyday lives. He calls us to change loyalties, redirect personal goals, turn away from our selfish past, and follow him with all of our hearts. The biblical word for this is *repent*. It simply means to make a 180 degree turn - like making a U-turn in your car. Following Jesus involves turning from your old way of life and moving toward a new way of life as a follower of the Lord.

This is the first and most crucial step to knowing God's plan for your life. Become a child of God. Be a follower of Christ. When you make the decision to follow Christ, your perspective changes. Suddenly, you realize that God has so much more in store for you.

It's the beginning of a great adventure.

CHAPTER 4

# BE FILLED

A driver's handbook. A written driving exam. The skills test with a strange examiner in the front seat with you. And the worst, parallel parking. Getting a driver's license can be a harrowing experience for some. But that is only the beginning for some teenagers. I recently spoke to a father who told me that his kids were not allowed to drive a car until they learned how to change a tire, change the oil, and jump off a car's dead battery.

There's one skill that all drivers need to know. If they don't have this skill, they can forget about driving a car. They have to know how to fill a car with gas. It's not that difficult, but I did recently see a lady circle the gas pumps several times trying to get her car's tank on the same side as the pumps!

It doesn't matter how good you score on your driving test. If you don't have fuel, you won't get anywhere. The same can be said for following Jesus. When we become followers of Jesus, we commit to following him daily as our Lord. But how do we do that? I've got good news. He fills us with his fuel. He fills us with his power. He fills us with his love. He fills us with all of his character qualities.

God's plan for your life is to be filled with his Holy Spirit.

> *Be very careful, then, how you live - not as unwise but as wise, making the most of every opportunity, because the days are evil. Therefore do not be foolish, but understand what the Lord's will is. Do not get drunk on wine, which leads to debauchery. Instead, be filled with the Spirit.*
>
> *- Ephesians 5:15-18*

This is from a letter that Paul the apostle wrote to the church in Ephesus (present day Turkey) in A.D. 61. It still applies to us today. There are a couple of things to note in this passage. First of all, it is foolish if we don't understand God's will. That's pretty strong. Nobody likes to be called a fool. Congratulations on choosing to read this book! Because you are discovering God's plan, you are not a fool.

There is something else to note in this letter. The last sentence is in the imperative tense in the Greek. In other words, it is a command, not a suggestion. *"Be filled with the Spirit."*

It sounds mystical and mysterious. What does it mean to be Spirit-filled? To be filled with God's Spirit means to yield your life to Christ and allow his presence and his personality to intervene in your life. To be filled with the Spirit is the next step as a Christ-follower. It is allowing him to be Lord of your life. Stepping aside and allowing God's Spirit to rule your life.

---

It is foolish if we don't understand God's will.

---

Maybe this will help. Suppose you have a pair of work gloves. Work gloves are designed to do work so you look at the gloves and say, "Okay, gloves, grab a shovel and dig a hole for me. Get to work!"

The gloves don't move.

Then you say, "Gloves, take a hammer and nail two pieces of wood together."

The gloves remain lifeless.

Maybe the gloves need inspiring. Maybe the gloves need to read a book on being a good glove. Maybe the gloves need to attend a small group with other gloves to learn how to live a successful life as a glove. Perhaps the gloves should find a podcast that will help them perform better. Or maybe the gloves could fly across the country and attend a conference for inspiration and teaching on gloveology.

No. What the gloves need in order to work are hands to go inside them. The gloves can't do work until hands go in and do the work through the gloves.

Maybe that's a silly illustration but here's the point. God's plan is to live his life through you. He wants you to live a supernatural life and the only way that can happen is to have his presence in you. We can't live the supernatural life of God in our strength. We need the power of God living in us through his Holy Spirit.

It is a constant spiritual exercise. Just as we admitted our sin, received his grace, and submitted ourselves to God at the beginning of our relationship with him, so we maintain that same attitude throughout our Christian walk. The life of a Christ follower not only begins with grace, but it continues in grace. We accept the duties and disciplines of the Christian life along the way, but our obedient responses spring from gratitude for the grace we have been given and continue to receive.

There's an old joke about a wife who asked her husband why he never says, "I love you." The husband explained to his bride, "I told you I loved you when I asked you to marry me. If I change my mind, I'll let you know."

We all know this is not the sign of a healthy marriage. A healthy marriage includes saying and showing love frequently. Being filled by the Spirit is a constant and frequent transaction between us and God. To live a Spirit-filled life is to consciously live each day in the awareness that we are marred by self-centeredness, and we need God's infinite and amazing grace to carry us through the day.

> The life of a Christ follower not only
> begins with grace, but it continues in grace.

The Greek word *pleroo* (pronounced play-ro-oh) is used of the wind filling the sail of a boat and moving it along. God's Holy Spirit is like the wind. We can't really see him, but we see the results. God's Spirit moves us along and gives us spiritual energy to live for him. To be filled with the Spirit is to be carried along from day to day, from moment to moment, from project to project, from thought to thought, from word to word, from deed to deed, by the power of the Spirit of God.

The person of the Holy Spirit convicts us when we stray away from God's plan for our lives (John 16:7-9). He counsels and helps us with godly wisdom (John 16:13-14), and he conforms us to the image of Christ revealing the nature of God in us.

This is God's will for you. Not doing so is foolish.

So how are we filled with God's Spirit? How do we fuel our lives with God's power? First, you must commit your life to Christ. You must be a follower of Christ as discussed in the previous chapter. Becoming a Christ-follower is transforming. It's a new way of living!

## DISCOVERING GOD'S PLAN

> *Anyone who belongs to Christ has become a new person. The old life is gone; a new life has begun!*
> *- 2 Corinthians 5:17, NLT*

Let God remake you and reshape the way you think. God's Spirit changes the way we think.

> *Don't copy the behavior and customs of this world, but let God transform you into a new person by changing the way you think. Then you will learn to know God's will for you, which is good and pleasing and perfect.*
> *- Romans 12:2, NLT*

We can think like God thinks when we read his Word, the Bible. The Bible is God's love letter to the world. When we make the Bible a part of our everyday life, i.e., reading it, studying it, and applying it to our lives, we learn how God thinks. When we learn about and practice spiritual disciplines such as prayer, worship, service, or stewardship, we are disciples of Jesus. As disciples of Jesus, we begin to think like him.

When we think like God thinks, we have a new mindset.

> *Those who live according to the flesh have their minds set on what the flesh desires; but those who live in accordance with the Spirit have their minds set on what the Spirit desires.*
> *- Romans 8:5*

You may be thinking, "Changing the way I think and having the right mindset? That doesn't sound very spiritual. It sounds more like pop psychology that I might find in a self-help book." The way you think is changed when you understand that God loves you, God forgives you, and God forgets your sin!

---

When we think like God thinks, we have a new mindset.

---

Do you remember the first time you fell in love? You really liked them but you weren't sure how they felt about you? You thought about it all the time. You wondered if they loved you. Then one day, they looked you deep in your eyes and said, "I love you." That's when you knew. That changed the way you thought about your relationship!

Jesus is taking you by the shoulders, looking deep in your eyes and saying, "I love you. In fact, I love you so much that I died for you." When you get that truth, the way you think changes.

Go back and read the last part of Romans 8:5. It says we should have our minds set on what the Spirit desires. What does the Spirit desire? That you bear His fruit. Bearing fruit is the next step in discovering God's plan for your life.

CHAPTER 5

# BE FRUITFUL

They say that the auto industry is changing in such a way that in the years to come, all of our cars are going to be self-driving cars. I don't know if I can sit in a car without myself or someone I trust behind the wheel. My question about self-driving cars is, what are teenagers going to look forward to if they don't have to learn how to drive a car?

Paul, the apostle who authored most of the New Testament books, wrote to the church in Galatia that they need to let the Holy Spirit take control of their lives. They need to let Jesus take the wheel. When the Holy Spirit guides us our lives are much fuller and richer. When we insist on being in control often times the wheels fall off.

In his letter to the church in Galatia, the apostle Paul encouraged the Christ-followers there to let the Holy Spirit guide them. Paul wrote that letter around A.D. 50. That was a long time ago, but it still applies to us today. We need to let the Holy Spirit guide our lives. When he is in charge of our lives, it is evident to us and others that God's Spirit has transformed us.

Being a follower filled with God's Spirit leads us to having the character of Christ in our lives. The character of Christ can be found throughout the New Testament, but an excellent summary of all of these character traits is found in Galatians 5.

> *The Holy Spirit produces this kind of fruit in our lives: love, joy, peace, patience, kindness, goodness, faithfulness, gentleness, and self-control.*
>
> *- Galatians 5:22-23, NLT*

The fruit of the Spirit is outward evidence of God's Spirit working in you. God's plan for you is that you bear fruit in your life. How do you know if you're filled with God's Spirit? The same way you know if you're eating a jelly filled doughnut. What's on the inside oozes out. If you're allowing God's Spirit to control your life, the fruit of the Spirit should be oozing out of you.

What if you had the fruit of the Spirit? What if you had the nine character traits that the apostle Paul wrote about in Galatians? You'd have the character of Jesus. And that is God's desire for you. God wants you to let his Holy Spirit guide you into a life of Christlikeness.

That's your purpose. You might not believe that there is a purpose for your life but I am here to tell you that if you have a pulse, you have a purpose. Everything has a purpose.

Do you love cockroaches? I'm going to guess your answer is no. But even cockroaches have a purpose. They help breakdown decaying wood and leaves and add nutrients to the soil through their waste. They are also a food source for small reptiles and mammals.

Do you love mosquitoes? Again, probably not. The purpose of mosquitoes is not to annoy humans but like bees and butterflies, they are actually pollinators. They transfer pollen from flower to flower as they feed on nectar, fertilizing plants and allowing them to form seeds and reproduce. Mosquitoes also serve as food for other creatures like birds and bats.

If cockroaches and mosquitoes have a purpose on this earth, then surely you do too!

God's main purpose for your life is to make you like Jesus Christ. The fruit of the Spirit isn't a list of what God wants you to DO. It's what God wants you to BE.

When we let the Holy Spirit guide our lives. He fills us with his fruit - which is Christlike character. Please understand. The fruit of the Spirit is the <u>result</u> of being filled and empowered by the Spirit, not the <u>means</u> of becoming filled with the Spirit. Don't look at this as a "to do list" of things you must do on your own in order to live like Christ. Look at this list as inspiration to live a Spirit-filled life. Wake up every day with your mind set on Christ. Determine to let his Holy Spirit guide you daily so that you can exhibit these Christlike qualities.

We also need to understand that God doesn't magically

zap us into Christlikeness. It's a process. It takes three to four years of growth for a peach tree to begin bearing fruit. We shouldn't be surprised then that it will take awhile for us to develop the fruit of the Spirit.

---

> The fruit of the Spirit isn't a list of what God wants you to DO. It's what God wants you to BE.

---

How do we go about the process of bearing fruit? It's about obedience and surrender. When we humble ourselves before God and let him take the wheel, the fruit of the Spirit will ooze out of our lives.

Note that love is the first fruit listed of the nine fruit in the passage above. Love is the foundation for the fruit of the Spirit. Jesus said the greatest thing we can do is love the Lord with all of our heart, mind, soul, and strength. The second greatest thing we can do is love others (Matthew 22:37-39). When you let love guide you, you'll be amazed at how love will help you bear the fruit of the Spirit.

Gene Jennings

---

When we humble ourselves before God and let him take the wheel, the fruit of the Spirit will ooze out of our lives.

---

Just as a branch on a vine produces fruit as it takes its nourishment from the vine, if we stay attached to Christ, he will continue to bear fruit in our lives. Jesus said it this way:

> *I am the true vine, and my Father is the gardener. He cuts off every branch in me that bears no fruit, while every branch that does bear fruit he prunes so that it will be even more fruitful. You are already clean because of the word I have spoken to you. Remain in me, as I also remain in you. No branch can bear fruit by itself; it must remain in the vine. Neither can you bear fruit unless you remain in me. I am the vine; you are the branches. If you remain in me and I in you, you will bear much fruit; apart from me you can do nothing… This is to my Father's glory, that you bear much fruit, showing yourselves to be my disciples.*
>
> *- John 15:1-5, 8*

Let me repeat what I wrote above: God's main purpose for your life is to make you like Jesus Christ. The fruit of the Spirit isn't a list of what God wants you to DO. It's what God wants you to BE.

Jesus said we would know his followers by their fruit. Followers of Jesus ought to have the character of Jesus.

CHAPTER 6

# BE A FAITHFUL SERVANT

At the end of every television show and movie, a list of credits comes across the screen. Sometimes they move so fast, it's impossible to read them all. Sometimes the credits are so small that even if they moved slow enough the words aren't big enough to read.

Hundreds of people work to entertain us for a thirty minute sitcom or a full-length movie. Behind every great show are a large number of skilled individuals who serve and support various parts of the production. They tirelessly work long days so the stars can shine. They know that their work will likely be under appreciated and unnoticed by those watching the show. But they do it anyway because they love being a part of creating something new. They enjoy serving on a team creating something larger than themselves.

The same is true with God's kingdom. In churches and ministries around the world, millions of people serve tirelessly to let those who don't know Jesus hear of his grace. Faithful servants provide care for the hurting, the needy, the lonely, and the disenfranchised. Believers serve the functions of churches and Christian organizations to promote and maintain their ministry. Christ followers use their gifts, abilities, talents, and experiences to make the good news of God's love known to all.

These millions of faithful Christian servants will likely never be recognized on earth. Credits will not roll across a screen at the end of their project. The Lead Pastor and musicians on stage may receive credit and recognition for a well done service but those behind the scenes are as important as those in front.

> *For it is God's will that by doing good you should silence the ignorant talk of foolish people. Live as free people, but do not use your freedom as a cover-up for evil; live as God's slaves.*
>
> *- 1 Peter 2:15-16*

> *You, my brothers and sisters, were called to be free. But do not use your freedom to indulge the flesh; rather, serve one another humbly in love.*
>
> *- Galatians 5:13*

> *Never be lacking in zeal, but keep your spiritual fervor, serving the Lord.*
>
> *- Romans 12:11*

Peter, a disciple of Jesus and author of several New Testament books, writes that it is God's will that we be faithful servants. God desires that we humbly serve others. A model Christ-follower should strive to be a help to those around them. Humble service is more than volunteering to help clean the church building or work in the church nursery every once in a while. Humble service is a 24/7 attitude. Remember, it's a mindset. We have our minds set on being faithful servants at home, at work, or in public settings. We want to be model citizens in our community and model employees at our jobs. God's plan for you is to be a submissive servant of Christ at all times. When we live good lives according to God's will, we "silence the ignorant talk of foolish men." In other words, unbelievers see Christ in us when we faithfully serve others.

God plans for us to be full-time missionaries. By that, I don't mean God wants you to quit your job, sign up with a missions organization, start asking your friends for financial support, move to the other side of the world, start speaking another language, and eat strange food. Being a missionary is not about location, it'a about identity. Missions isn't something we do, it's something we are. We are all missionaries with different assignments in various locations. For sure, some Christ-followers are called to leave the comforts of their home and move to an impoverished part of the world. This is important work and God needs more workers around the globe. But it's not for everyone. Some Christ-followers are "goers." Others stay back to serve locally and support those who are doing the work globally.

# DISCOVERING GOD'S PLAN

God plans for us to be full-time missionaries.

God is a missionary God. The Bible is the story of God reaching out to others and revealing himself to the world. It is clear that God loves everyone, and he desires that everyone discover his plan. We are missionaries because we follow a missionary God. How you serve as a missionary in our world is part of God's plan for your life. As you discover God's plan, you may find yourself on an airplane some day beginning a new adventure serving God in a foreign land, or you may find yourself serving God in your hometown. Whether across the street or across the globe, we are to be on mission as faithful servants of God.

The apostle Paul also wrote a letter to the church in Corinth. He writes that, as believers, we are Christ's ambassadors (2 Corinthians 5:20). Ambassadors are representatives of a higher power. An ambassador at the United Nations represents his or her home country and it's leadership. The ambassador serves to act on behalf of the nation they are called to serve.

As his ambassadors, God wants us to live as Spirit-filled, fruit bearing servants in this world. He designed us to be used. We work to expand God's kingdom by serving his

Church, our communities, and our world. We do not work to earn our salvation. Our salvation comes by grace alone. We work because of grace not for grace.

For many years my family enjoyed boating. When I was young, we spent many hours water-skiing and tubing at a large lake near our home. My dad would pull my friends and me around the lake for hours and hours. Later as a dad myself, I sat behind the helm of the boat pulling my children and their friends until we were all water-logged and sunburned.

As the kids got older, the boat was used less. When they left home to go away to college, the boat sat unused for over a year. Boats aren't designed to sit under carports collecting dust. They need to be used. When a boat sits up for too long, the gas in the fuel lines begin to gel. The vinyl seats begin to dry rot. Mold and mildew begin to appear. Eventually, when a boat sits on land for too long it falls into disrepair. Boats are best kept in shape by being used frequently.

Christ followers are designed to be used. God wants you to be a faithful servant. When Christ followers are faithfully serving their church and their world, they find energy, calling, passion, and love. Christ followers who choose not to use their gifts, talents, abilities, and experiences to serve are like boats abandoned on dry land.

> *Each of you should use whatever gift you have received to serve others, as faithful stewards of God's grace in its various forms.*
>
> *- 1 Peter 4:10*

Why do we serve? First of all, we primarily serve God

not men. We serve as an expression of thanks for the amazing grace God has provided to us through Jesus Christ. We serve God out of gratitude for how he has transformed our lives. We do not serve because we feel that we must serve to make God happy with us. We serve because we want to serve.

We also serve to start a ministry or sustain a ministry. Ministries require work. Our main purpose as followers of Jesus is to make disciples of all nations. This is the command Jesus gave us in Matthew 28:19-20:

*Go and make disciples of all nations, baptizing them in the name of the Father and of the Son and of the Holy Spirit, and teaching them to obey everything I have commanded you. And surely I am with you always, to the very end of the age.*

Making disciples is no simple process. It could be as easy as one friend sharing the good news of Jesus with a friend. This is how my life was changed. When I asked a friend of mine about his relationship with God, he shared the gospel with me and my life has never been the same.

---

We serve as an expression of thanks for the amazing grace God has provided to us through Jesus Christ.

Making disciples can often be a multifaceted approach. If I wanted to share the gospel with someone from another culture who speaks another language, it will take some time and energy for me to share with that person on a level they can understand. In this case, years of language study may be necessary. Becoming friends and earning the trust of others could take months - even years. Ministry requires work.

My grandmother-in-law was one of the most humble servants of God I've ever known. She lived a very simple life. It seemed she spent most of her life in the kitchen or at a sewing machine. She cooked hundreds of meals for her church family for over two decades. Everyone loved Nanny's cooking. Every Wednesday night her church offered a meal for busy families, and every Wednesday she served them. While I'm sure some people thanked her for preparing a meal, overall it was a thankless job. But Nanny didn't cook for the masses for a pat on the back. She cooked because she loved her Lord, his church, and her church family.

Nanny used her gifts to serve others. She used her God-given skills to serve the body of Christ. The apostle Paul described the Church as the body of Christ in which we all have a part to play in the mission.

*Just as a body, though one, has many parts, but all its many parts form one body, so it is with Christ. For we were all baptized by one Spirit so as to form one body—whether Jews or Gentiles, slave or free—and we were all given the one Spirit to drink. Even so the body is not made up of one part but of many.*

*Now if the foot should say, "Because I am not a hand, I do not belong to the body," it would not for that reason stop being part of the body. And if the ear should say, "Because I am not an eye, I do not belong to the body," it would not for that reason stop being part of the body. If the whole body were an eye, where would the sense of hearing be? If the whole body were an ear, where would the sense of smell be? But in fact God has placed the parts in the body, every one of them, just as he wanted them to be. If they were all one part, where would the body be? As it is, there are many parts, but one body.*

*The eye cannot say to the hand, "I don't need you!" And the head cannot say to the feet, "I don't need you!" On the contrary, those parts of the body that seem to be weaker are indispensable, and the parts that we think are less honorable we treat with special honor. And the parts that are unpresentable are treated with special modesty, while our presentable parts need no special treatment. But God has put the body together, giving greater honor to the parts that lacked it, so that there should be no division in the body, but that its parts should have equal concern for each other. If one part suffers, every part suffers with it; if one part is honored, every part rejoices with it. Now you are the body of Christ, and each one of you is a part of it.*

*- 1 Corinthians 12:12-27*

This is a beautiful picture of how the Church works. When believers use their gifts, talents, and experiences to faithfully serve each other and the world around them, the love of Jesus is made known, the gospel is made clear, and people are transformed. Whether you serve as an ear, a foot, or a kidney, we all have a part to play as a servant in the body of Christ.

Dwight L. Moody, a famous 19th century pastor, once said, "The measure of a man is not how many servants he has, but how many men he serves." God has designed us to humbly serve. This is God's plan for your life.

CHAPTER 7

# PUTTING IT ALL TOGETHER: FREEDOM

A farmer wrestled in his mind whether he should plant corn in his fields or plant wheat instead. He couldn't make up his mind so he knelt in the middle of his land and prayed, "Lord, I'm not sure what I should do. I always want to be obedient to you and do your will. Please help me know what you want me to do with my life."

After he prayed, the farmer lifted his eyes to the heavens and miraculously saw two clouds form the letters P and C. "PC? The farmer thought? What is the Lord trying to tell me?" After a moment, the farmer had a revelation. "PC means Preach Christ!"

The farmer ran home and told his wife, "God has called me to be a preacher!" His wife was stunned but she submitted to her husband's calling. Within weeks, they sold the farm, moved to a tiny apartment in the city, and the farmer enrolled in Bible College. He began studying Greek and Hebrew. He learned all kinds of multisyllabic theological terms. But he was miserable. He was made for the farm not the classroom.

His wife and family weren't happy either. They didn't like living in a cramped apartment in the city. They wanted to be back in the wide open spaces where they belonged.

The farmer was discouraged. He thought he was doing exactly what God wanted him to do. Late one night, while laboring through a theology textbook in the college library, he bowed his head and prayed. "Lord, I asked you in the field a few months ago what I should do with my life, and you clearly and miraculously gave me a sign in the sky. PC - Preach Christ. But this is hard, Lord. I'm discouraged. My family is depressed. Should I continue on? Is this really what you want me to do with my life?"

At that point, the farmer witnessed another miracle. It was the audible voice of God. "When I formed the letters P and C in the clouds that day, I didn't intend for you to preach Christ. I was trying to tell you to plant corn."

Like the farmer, sometimes we make following God's plan for our lives more mystical and mysterious than it has to be. This chapter is my favorite. It's the best part of understanding God's plan. Like putting all of the pieces of a puzzle together, God's plan for you becomes clearer when you put together everything you've read to this point.

God wants you to follow Christ. He wants you to be filled with his Spirit. He wants you to produce spiritual fruit, and he wants you to serve him faithfully. These four things must be in place in your life. You don't have to be perfect.

You will always be working on these qualities throughout your life. These are things you will pursue in your walk with God each and every day.

So, you're probably asking at this point, "How do I know where to go to college? How do I know God's will about the relationship that I'm in? How do I know God's will about my career decision? How do I know God's will about that business deal? What should I do with my retirement years? What about my future? How does this help me make practical everyday decisions for my life?"

That's the best part. If you are living according to the four principles above, the last principle is: God frees us to do whatever our heart desires.

Think about it. If you are living according to the four principles, who is in control of your life? God is! When you are a faithful, fruitful, Spirit-filled follower, you are living exactly as God intended for you to live!

> *Take delight in the Lord, and he will give you the desires of your heart.*
>
> *- Psalm 37:4*

When you are delighting in the Lord, the desires in your heart are God-given. Your heart's desires are no longer your desires. They are God's desires for your life. He placed them there for you. God makes the desires of your heart attainable when you've given your life to him.

There is merit to the saying, "Follow your heart." But there is a caveat. Follow your heart when you are faithfully following Christ. The prophet Jeremiah wrote that the heart is deceitful (Jeremiah 17:9). It can't always be trusted. Proverbs 28:26 says he who trusts in his own mind is a fool.

*Trust in the Lord with all your heart and lean not on your own understanding; in all your ways submit to him, and he will make your paths straight.*

*- Proverbs 3:5-6*

In order to follow our hearts, our lives must be fully submitted to the Lord. Every morning we should decide that the Lord is going to have our day. Before we roll out of bed at dawn, give the day to Jesus. As we shuffle our way to the coffeepot in the kitchen, determine that today is God's day. While we're going out the door to face the day, face it with Jesus walking ahead of you - leading the way. When we arrive at the school, office, factory, or wherever we spend most of our days, live as a faithful, fruitful, Spirit-filled follower of Jesus Christ, and he will place his desires in our hearts. When we are living in total surrender and in complete union with God, we are free to act on the desires of our heart because God put them there.

Here's a key principle to grasp. Understand the following two sentences and you'll understand God's will for your life.

*God's plan for your life is more about the person God wants you to be, not just the place he wants you to be. It's more about character than career.*

You can be a dairy farmer or a doctor. A steel worker or a stock broker. A plumber or a pilot. A teacher or a truck driver. You can do whatever your heart desires - just do it with Jesus. The main thing is having Christ in you. God will take you and your interests, your personality, your talents, your gifts, and your abilities and put you in the right place if you put him in first place.

---

> When we are living in total surrender and in complete union with God, we are free to act on the desires of our heart because God put them there.

---

When I was a young man and a new follower of Jesus, there was a wonderful layman in our church. I'll call him Mr. Henry. Mr. Henry was a humble and selfless servant of the Lord. He was a mainstay at almost every service or event. He never attended Bible college or seminary. He wasn't formally trained to do ministry. Other than serving as a deacon in the church, he had no special titles, skills, or positions. He was a simple servant of God. He served in multiple capacities at the church. He used his vacation time to lead an annual mission trip to an impoverished community in Appalachia. But more than just serving at the church, he served and ministered to people throughout our community. He built handicapped ramps for the elderly and those with special needs. He was a member of several community service organizations. He assisted with the local sports programs. He helped his wife start a restaurant, and he helped his son open a sporting goods store - at the same time. All while working his own full time job. It seemed like he was everywhere all the time helping other people. In the midst of it all, he raised a fine family who remain faithful to each other and the Lord to this day.

Knowing that Mr. Henry was an outstanding servant of God for many, many years, I will never forget the opening line of the pastor's eulogy at his funeral. "He was a potato chip salesman."

Mr. Henry worked for a local food distributor that supplied potato chips to local grocery stores and convenience stores. His career in life was selling potato chips, but his calling in life was showing the love of Christ through service. He made an impact on literally hundreds of people over his lifetime. He did it because he loved God, and he wanted others to know the God he loved.

Mr. Henry discovered God's plan for his life. He lived his life as a faithful, fruitful, Spirit-filled follower of Christ. He delighted in the Lord, and he followed the desires of his heart. Mr. Henry's natural desire was to help people. He was in his sweet spot when he was serving. He was always looking for an opportunity to help others. When his heart went out to a person in need or a notable cause in the community, he did what he could to help fill the need.

And he is sorely missed today.

Doing God's will is good, pleasing, and perfect. When

you are living as a faithful, fruitful, Spirit-filled follower, you are in your sweet spot.

> *Do not conform to the pattern of this world, but be transformed by the renewing of your mind. Then you will be able to test and approve what God's will is - his good, pleasing and perfect will.*
>
> *- Romans 12:2*

Do you want to live a good life? Follow God's good plan for your life. Do you want to live a life that is pleasing to you and God? Follow God's good plan for your life. Do you want to be in God's perfect will? Follow God's plan. Live your life as a devoted follower of Jesus. Let the fruit of his Holy Spirit bloom and blossom in your life. Remember the fruit of the Spirit is love, joy, peace, patience, kindness, goodness, faithfulness, gentleness, and self-control (Galatians 5:22-23). Finally, be a faithful servant of God. Serve God by serving your family, your friends, your church family, your co-workers, your neighbors, and your community. When you are living your life in this way, you are living according to God's plan for your life.

Still not sure what to do next? Focus on being a faithful, fruitful, Spirit-filled follower and God will show you which way to go.

> *Take delight in the Lord, and he will give you the desires of your heart.*
>
> *- Psalm 37:4*

CHAPTER 8

# MORE THAN YOU COULD ASK OR IMAGINE

What are your dreams for your life? To find a spouse? To settle into a new career? To be a professional athlete? To own your own business? To be a medical worker, teacher, builder, architect, or some other respectable form of employment? To be a world-renowned musician? To be a mother? To be a missionary?

If you are living as a faithful, fruitful, Spirit-filled follower of Jesus, you are free to pursue those things. But understand this. God's dreams for your life are much bigger than your dreams. You probably wouldn't believe what God has in store for you if he told you. The apostle Paul wrote that God is able to do much more than we could ask for or even imagine!

> *Now to him who is able to do immeasurably more than all we ask or imagine, according to his*

# DISCOVERING GOD'S PLAN

*power that is at work within us, to him be glory in the church and in Christ Jesus throughout all generations, for ever and ever! Amen.*

*- Ephesians 3:20-21*

I had great dreams and plans for my life after I graduated seminary. I was running down a dream. My dream. But God's dreams for my life were so much bigger and better than anything I could ever imagine. I never could have orchestrated the things God has done in my life. God fulfilled my dreams and then heaped on his dreams for my life. The things I dreamed for were small compared to the dreams God had for me. My dreams in metro Atlanta didn't come true. In hindsight, I wasn't prepared for those dreams. I needed time to learn, grow, and mature. If God had fulfilled my dreams for my church in Atlanta, I would not have been able to handle it. I was too young, too green, and too inexperienced.

---

God's dreams for your life are much bigger than your dreams.

---

God knew exactly what I needed, where I needed to go, and who I needed to go with me. As I reflect on my past, I am amazed at God's timing. What some might call coincidence, I call miracles. While some may say I manufactured my own circumstances, I say I'm not that smart. What some may call luck, I call blessing. The joy of living as a faithful, fruitful, Spirit-filled follower of Jesus Christ each day brings about the most abundant life you can never imagine. You can't imagine it! You just have to wait for it, and God will fulfill his plans for you at just the right time.

> *Let us not become weary in doing good, for at the proper time we will reap a harvest if we do not give up.*
>
> *- Galatians 6:9*

My pastor and friend, Steve Davis, calls this life "following the breadcrumbs." The idea of following the breadcrumbs originates in the German fairy tale of Hansel and Gretel. To avoid getting lost and to find their way home while walking in the woods, Hansel left behind a trail of breadcrumbs. Steve uses this term to describe following God. We live the life we know he wants us to live. We live humbly, obediently, lovingly, and faithfully. We apply the four principles to our everyday life. As God reveals people or circumstances in our lives that meet the desires of our hearts, we consider that a breadcrumb. We take it and go in the direction of the breadcrumb to see where God takes us. Most of the time, it's more than we could dream or imagine! God directs the steps of his faithful followers.

# DISCOVERING GOD'S PLAN

*The mind of man plans his way, but the Lord directs his steps.*

*- Proverbs 16:9, NASB*

As you go about the adventurous life of following Jesus, may you go with boldness, courage, hope, faith, and love. Live your life in the way that God designed for you to live. Follow the breadcrumbs as he drops them in front of you, and you will be amazed at what God will do with ordinary you!

# Notes

1. Yandall Woodfin, *Why Be A Christian?* (Nashville, TN: Broadman Press, 1988), p. 14
2. Michael Green, *Illustrations for Biblical Preaching*, (Grand Rapids, MI: Baker Book House, 1989), p. 329

# About the Author

Gene Jennings has been a pastor since 1987 having served churches in Texas, Georgia, and South Carolina. He has traveled as a missionary and speaker in many other states as well as Australia, Costa Rica, Guatemala, Indonesia, Mexico, St. Croix, Tanzania, and the Middle East. Gene is the Associate Pastor at TrueNorth Church in North Augusta, South Carolina. He is a graduate of the University of South Carolina at Aiken and Southwestern Baptist Theological Seminary in Fort Worth, Texas. He lives in North Augusta with his wife, Beth, and their dog, Roadie. He has a son, Cliff, and a daughter-in-law, Amanda, a daughter, Bailey, and a son-in-law, Kyle. Gene has four grandchildren, Elijah, Emersyn, Sanders, Kinsley, and one more on the way!

If you enjoyed *Discovering God's Plan*,
please buy one for a friend!

Made in the USA
Columbia, SC
27 May 2021